WIT AND WISDOM

To Lauren,

"She is more precious
than rubies ..."
Proverbs 3:15

Rev. A. Coutts Rice

WIT AND WISDOM

Lessons on Life, Love, and Leadership

A. COLETTE RICE

WIT AND WISDOM
LESSONS ON LIFE, LOVE, AND LEADERSHIP

iUniverse books may be ordered through booksellers or by contacting:

iUniverse
1663 Liberty Drive
Bloomington, IN 47403
www.iuniverse.com
1-800-Authors (1-800-288-4677)

ISBN: 978-1-5320-6183-7 (sc)
ISBN: 978-1-5320-6181-3 (hc)
ISBN: 978-1-5320-6182-0 (e)

Library of Congress Control Number: 2018913855

Print information available on the last page.

iUniverse rev. date: 04/11/2019

To God—You are the lifter of my head!

In loving memory of my parents, Ned and Sarah Rice, for nourishing me richly from their deep well of wisdom. While the pain of missing them is often unbearable, the indelible imprint their deposits made on my life serve as a daily reminder that they are always with me.

To my big baby sister, Toniere, whose courage fascinates me and whose heart for me sustains my faith in unconditional love.

To my muse, Tarryn, whose love, friendship, and fresh perspective energize me beyond measure.

To my tribe—you *all* know who you are—who encourage me, inspire me, and help me to be the best me I can be.

Love you!

.

In those homely sayings was couched the
collective wisdom of generations.
—Maya Angelou

Happy are those who find wisdom, and
those who get understanding.
—Proverbs 3:13 NRSV

CONTENTS

INTRODUCTION

A Heap See, but Few Know

In a conversation with my wise ol' uncle Ben one hot sunny afternoon as we sat rocking on his porch, I commented on a situation based on what I saw and confidently thought I knew. As we watched a young woman in her early twenties walk down the road struggling to manage bags of groceries with her five children in tow, I remarked that her apparent woes must have been attributed to a lifestyle of poor choices and loose living. He quickly noted that my commentary was way off base, but rather than saying outright, "You are wrong," he responded with "Colette, a heap see, but few know." I just paused as my young, immature mind silently wondered what in the world he was talking about. While it was a little too deep for me to process at the time, I did have sense enough to know he had just said *something*—and that that *something* had value. I never forgot what he said to me on the porch that day. It remained in the back of my mind.

It would be many, many years later, after Dad, Mom, and Uncle Ben had all passed, that I found myself once again on that same porch, sitting in that same rocking chair, on the day of Uncle Ben's home-going service after having had the privilege of preaching his eulogy. I rocked and pondered the many things in life that remained such a mystery to me, the things I thought I understood but really had not grasped at all, and then it hit me—those same words he had uttered many, many years before were ringing vividly in my ears: "A heap see, but few know." But this time, it made all the sense in the world. He was trying to teach me the importance of truly understanding. In my aha moment, the revelation was short and sweet. Simply put, many have eyesight, but few have insight.

As I think back over my life, I see that I was blessed to have my parents and other people in my life who had never been afforded the opportunity to pursue a college education and yet were steeped in rich wisdom and quick wit. Their invaluable deposits have helped mold, shape, and make me the woman I am today.

I truly believe there is truth in the saying "The fruit doesn't fall far from the tree." This never became more abundantly clear than when I began to acknowledge how often I preface every other statement with "My mother used to always say" or "My father used to tell me all the time." These are followed by some witty remark, words of wisdom, or a word to the wise that I have held on to and now find myself attempting to pass on to others.

According to Dictionary.com, *wit* means "the keen perception and cleverly apt expression of those connections between ideas that awaken amusement and pleasure; speech or writing showing such perception and expression." And the *American Heritage Dictionary of English Language* defines *wisdom* as "the sum of learning through the ages; knowledge; wise teachings of the ancient sages."

While it is indeed important to continue with this oral tradition, my dad used to say, "The shortest pencil is longer than the longest memory." Bearing his words in mind, I have found great joy in pausing to compile these thoughts, sayings, and words of wisdom, many of which you may have heard or even said yourself—some familiar and others perhaps not so familiar. Glean what you can, and disregard the rest. Or, in other words, as I always say, "Chew up the meat and spit out the bones." My prayer for this book is that those who have ears to hear will continue to pass down the wisdom of our forebears and that these lessons on life, love, and leadership will help to positively impact and empower a new generation. Enjoy!

SECTION 1

LIFE

CHAPTER 1

LASTING IMPACT

Keep the Main Thing the Main Thing

All too often, if we are not careful, we can allow ourselves to be sidetracked by the rabbit trails of life. If we choose to wander down those trails, they will distract us from meeting our goals and fulfilling our purpose and may stall our journeys. Staying focused on the main thing will help keep us on track for destiny.

Time Heals All Wounds; Give Time Some Time

When life's disappointments, trials, and even tragedies befall us, we often feel as though there is no way we can get past the trauma. However, time has a way of making things better. We should just allow time some time!

The Shortest Pencil Is Longer Than the Longest Memory

Even as a child, I remember how I would get a set of instructions from my parents and forget soon (if not immediately) after it left their lips and hit my ears. I would walk away and return quickly, uttering the words "What was it again?" My father would reply, "Write it down. Don't you know that the shortest pencil is longer than the longest memory?" I've now fully embraced the practice of writing things down, realizing that as I have grown a little older, my memory is growing shorter.

Treasure Your Gifts and Give Them Freely

All of us have been endowed with something special that is specifically intended to be used to bless someone else. Within us is the answer to a question, the ability to meet a need, the solution to a problem, or the cure to an ill. Your gifts may be revealed as you observe the things that make your heart smile and explore the things that you are passionate about, do well, and operate in naturally. Whatever you do, do not rest until you find your gift and give of it freely so that others may benefit from the blessing.

A Smile Is a Situation Changer

Smiling has medical benefits. According to Dr. Ronald E. Riggio in an article in *Psychology Today*, "The act of smiling activates neural messaging that benefits your health and happiness." A smile can be a mood changer, a situation diffuser, a spirit lifter, a communication-barrier breaker, and even a peacemaker. Try smiling rather than frowning; the outcome will amaze you when you turn that frown upside down.

True Friendships Should Be Treasured

My mother taught me at a very young age that true friends were hard to come by. She believed genuine friendship was so rare that in a lifetime I would likely be able to count them on one hand. As usual, she was right. When God brings friends into your life who are loyal, loving, and true, know they are a treasure.

Relationships Need to Be Nourished

In the busyness of life, we often neglect those closest to us. Albeit unintentionally, we take for granted that they will always be there. Yet few things are more precious in life than those who are placed in our inner circles whose presence is designed to help in some way to perfect us for our purpose. These relationships need to be nourished so we can flourish.

If You Hang around the Garbage Pail, You Will Start Smelling like Trash

It is very interesting how easily we are influenced, sometimes subliminally, by the people with whom we associate. Over time, you can start to pick up their mannerisms, traits, and even habits, both good and bad. Therefore, a word to the wise—be mindful and watchful of the company you keep.

If Your Money Holds Out, Your Luck Is Bound to Change

This is a gambling metaphor that essentially means that if players can remain in the game, their losing streak will eventually turn around. So it is with the game of life; one must be determined to hang in there during the difficult seasons because trouble doesn't last forever!

No Good Deed Goes Unpunished

Interjecting yourself into a situation to assist is noble and can yield great reward. However, be sure that you consider it wisely and prayerfully before you do. For example, imagine that a friend shares with you that he needs a temporary place to stay. You offer him your spare bedroom, and a year later, he is still there. Know that there will be times when attempts to help will come with more attached than you bargained for.

Water Seeks Its Own Level

This figuratively suggests that people seek out others to be around who they perceive to be like them. Therefore, it is important to be discerning about whom you choose and whom you allow to choose you. Always remember that you will be judged by the company you keep.

The Leaning Tree Isn't Always the First to Fall

Sometimes we make assumptions about the incompetency or presumed weaknesses of others. However, don't be fooled about their potential to hang in there and sometimes outlast those who, by all accounts, appear stronger. Appearances are deceiving. When the dust settles, the one leaning may be the last one standing.

Don't Cut off Your Nose to Spite Your Face

Taking a hard-nosed approach when conflicts arise is not the best stance if you are seeking resolution. A stubborn approach is often a risky gamble. You could wind up forcing an impasse and possibly losing even more than you expected.

You Can't Judge a Book by Its Cover

We sometimes have the tendency to look at the cover of a book and determine, irrespective of the content, whether it is going to be worth our time or not. If we are not careful, we can find ourselves applying this same methodology to other areas of life, including things, people, and even opportunities. We must see beyond the surface to fully evaluate and appreciate the things that come our way.

Show Up as the Teacher or the Student—Just Show Up

The practice of being present is one that requires great discipline to develop. When you give the right attention to being fully present for every encounter, you will generally find one of two things: that you are the teacher, wherein you may be used to impart, or you are the student, wherein you find opportunity to glean and receive impartation. You are apt to miss an amazing blessing if you don't practice presence. Whatever you do, just show up!

When You Play with a Dog, He Will Lick Your Mouth at the Most Inopportune Time

There are times when we let our guard down and get comfortable with others. When doing so, we find ourselves accepting behavior, comments, and so on that would ordinarily be unacceptable; we just let it slide. However, it is not until you enter a public setting when the same dog that you played with, laughed with, and trusted turns on you, embarrassing or humiliating you when least expected and at the most inopportune moment. Watch how you interact with the company you keep in private because it may become public in ways you cannot anticipate.

Hindsight Is Twenty-Twenty

Twenty-twenty is the rating given to those who have been determined to have near-perfect vision. It always amazes me how much clearer things are when I look back at a situation versus when I am in the midst of it. While it would be wonderful to have insight when faced with every circumstance, life doesn't always afford us that clarity. It is more likely that it will be when we look back, rather than when we look at the situation, that our vision will be clear.

Stop Majoring in Minors
and Minoring in Majors

On my list of top-five favorite movies is *Point of No Return* staring Bridget Fonda. One of lines in the movie that impacted me most was when her refining coach made her repeat the phrase "I never mind much about the little things." The coach was training her how to prioritize the issues of life. How much further along in life might we all be if we learned how to deemphasize the insignificant and instead major in what really matters most?

Don't Let the Devil Ride, or He'll Want to Drive

As you journey through life, always remember there are adversarial forces in place that seek to keep you from purpose and promise. Be careful not to allow any room for the enemy to come in. Once he does, he will most assuredly want to pull up a chair and sit center stage in the arena of your life. Don't give way to evil, but overcome evil with good.

CHAPTER 2

LIMITATIONS

The Juice Just Isn't Worth the Squeeze

Just because you are right about something does not mean you must press your point on the matter. In many instances, you will learn that every potential battle does not have to be fought. I often counsel couples whose insistence on being right has led to long, drawn-out fights that could have easily been avoided. Oftentimes, it is much better to hold your peace. If you don't, you may find that the outcome of the pressing your point is not worth the effort. Let it rest!

Money Doesn't Grow on Trees

Some people, particularly children, seem to believe that there is an endless supply of resources. The imagery is that of a tree in the backyard that produces money on a whim, and all you have to do is shake it. All hardworking parents have a responsibility to dispel such a myth by teaching their children about the origin of money and how to manage it so that they don't enter adulthood thinking that there is a money tree somewhere.

Cut Your Coat According to Your Cloth

It is wise and prudent to consider your budget to avoid the pitfalls of overspending. Spending beyond your means could land you deep in debt. When making financial decisions, do not overextend yourself, but rather work within your means.

Talk Is Cheap; It Takes Money to Buy Land

It can be somewhat frustrating and perhaps even irritating to deal with people who are always talking but never producing. Don't be that kind of individual; it is not flattering. Other ways to say this phrase are "Rather than talk about it, be about it," "Put your money where your mouth is," and "Put up or shut up!"

You Must Make a Deposit before You Can Make a Withdrawal

There is no way you can walk into a bank with a zero account balance and demand a withdrawal. Likewise, you cannot make demands on others with whom you have not yet made a deposit. Always remember the universal law that dictates that where there is sowing, reaping is sure to follow.

Hope for the Best, Expect the Worst, and Take Whatever Comes

Hope helps us to face each new day, sustains us as we encounter trials in life, and catapults us to accomplish our goals. Anticipating challenges is one of the greatest cushions to the blow of disappointment, and acceptance of circumstances beyond our control brings unmeasurable peace, even in the worst situations.

Believe Half of What You See and None of What You Hear

Things are not always as they appear. For instance, you may notice that a woman is crying and assume that she is sad, when in fact she may have laughed so hard that she was moved to tears. Don't hinge your wages on what you think you see, because the situation may not actually be as it seems. Furthermore, by sharing information, something is bound to be lost in translation, especially when it comes to gossip passed through the grapevine. Don't believe it; rarely is it reliable.

Don't Put More on Your Plate Than You Can Say Grace Over

One of the biggest challenges in life is learning how to avoid taking on more than we can handle. When this goes unmanaged, it greatly impedes optimum performance, thereby compromising success. Part of being successful in life is learning the art of choosing the best yes and learning how to unapologetically say no. Once you've mastered this, you will be better positioned to live life on purpose to fulfill your purpose.

Never Ask a Naked Man for
the Clothes off His Back

There will be times in life when you will have to negotiate with others to resolve an issue, meet a need, or secure a special accommodation. Never try to accomplish this by dealing with someone who is not empowered to address your situation to your satisfaction. It is a waste of time. Whenever you get a no, always ask the question "Who has the authority to say yes?" That is who you want to be in conversation with.

If the Lord's Willing and the Creek Don't Rise

Men and women of their word are committed to keeping promises. However, we all know that, despite our best efforts to be faithful to our word, life has a way of happening in between our plans. This caveat attached to a commitment communicates the sentiment that the promise is good unless some unforeseeable circumstance or impenetrable barrier should arise to prevent the promise from being fulfilled.

You Are Always the Last Person to Smell Yourself

Odd but true! If you wear perfume and fragrances the way they should be worn, you generally won't smell yourself. That is because your sweet, savory scent is primarily designed to benefit those who grace your presence and cross your path. Unfortunately, the converse is true with smells that are not so pleasant, like when the perfume is overbearing, when your breath smells unpleasant, or when your deodorant has long since worn off. If you smell yourself, it is too late.

If a Frog Had Wings, He Wouldn't Bump His Butt

Obsessing over things that cannot be changed is both futile and unproductive. The effort and energy placed in the "If I would have," "If I could have," and "If I had just" thoughts surrounding any given situation only have value to the extent that we embrace the lessons learned. Beyond that, the best thing to do is to accept what cannot be changed.

If It Doesn't Fit, Don't Force It!

We need to resist the temptation to push our own agenda. When things are not working out like we would like them to, it doesn't necessarily mean they are not working for our ultimate good. Don't hold on to your own desires with too tight a rein. Learn when it is time to let go.

Out of the Frying Pan into the Fire

When you jump out of the frying pan into the fire, you are making a bad situation worse. The heat from the pan is at least a controllable heat. Use wisdom in choosing your next words and your next move. Once you're in the fire, the heat rises to another level, and you are bound to get burned!

Your Eyes Are Bigger
Than Your Stomach

This is often said when people are being greedy when preparing to eat a meal. They put a lot a food on their plates without considering how much they will be able to eat. The result is food left over and wasted. Don't make the mistake of wasting time by putting more on the plate of life than you can handle.

You Can't Make Happenings When There Ain't None

This is a valuable lesson I learned as a young teenager when my bestie and I were trying to play hooky with a boy we liked. The plan was to meet up at his house, but it fell through when his mother decided to stay home from work. We were so disappointed when he delivered the news. We pressed for an alternative plan, but his response was this bead of wisdom that I have held on to for years since. I shudder to think of what unfortunate possibilities could have resulted from our getting our way. Whether it is matters of life, love, or labor, be careful not to press too hard or insist on your agenda, particularly when things are not falling into place like you hoped. It very well could be they were not intended to work out. Be open to that possibility.

You Can't Squeeze Blood out of a Turnip

It is important to acknowledge when your efforts are fruitless. This is inevitable when you seek after something from someone that they are unable to give. Try as hard as you may, you'll never get blood from a turnip because blood is something that the turnip is incapable of yielding, no matter how hard you try.

CHAPTER 3

LISTENING

Know When You Know

All too often, we instinctively know something, yet we second-guess ourselves only to get to the end of our rope and utter the all-too-familiar words "I knew it!" Many of life's lessons would be a lot less painful if we just trusted our inner voices and followed the advice to "know when we know."

Believe What You Know

It is very interesting how we can know something and yet not embrace it in our own lives. For example, most people know that a consistent exercise regimen is good for their health, yet many people don't have one. It is not enough to simply have knowledge of a thing. We must truly believe in what we know to make a difference. When we believe what we know, great and amazing things become possible.

Always Seek to Find the Redemptive Value

I have come to the place in life where I seek to approach every situation, particularly the unpleasant ones, with one prayer on my lips and one question in mind. I pray to God to show me the light, and I ask, "What is the redemptive value?" I once had to deal with an extremely difficult and unreasonable employee who challenged me on every turn. While trying at the time, the experience taught me how to exercise self-control and strengthened my leadership skills. I now understand that I inevitably find the lesson God intended me to learn when I seek to find it.

A Dog That Will Bring a Bone Will Carry a Bone

Be leery of people, well meaning or otherwise, who are talebearers and information carriers. Resist the temptation to share your innermost thoughts, personal business, or private musings. Chances are—if they brought something that they shouldn't have to you, they will likely take something they shouldn't to someone else. Beware of the bone bringers!

Chew up the Meat and Spit out the Bones

When I was much younger, I completely tuned out people I didn't like, didn't understand, or assumed had nothing to offer. Consequently, I missed out on countless opportunities to learn, grow, and glean from people who didn't necessarily think, talk, or act like I did. However, my eyes were opened once I attended seminary, exposing me to so many people from varying walks of life who, while different from me, manifested amazing gifts as communicators that truly arrested my attention. I have since learned that all encounters have growth potential and deposit possibilities. I now keep an open mind and have learned to listen, taking what I can use and leaving what I can't.

We Rarely See Ourselves as Others Do

This is something my father would always say to me, and how true it is! Take a moment to ask your trusted friends, loved ones, and confidants how *they* see you through *their* eyes. It will likely be a cathartic experience when you hear what they have to say—the good and the bad. We seldom see ourselves as others do.

CHAPTER 4

LIBERATION

Celebrate the Gift of You

When God made you, He broke the mold. Of the billions of people who have lived on earth, both past and present, not one shares your exact DNA. You are a designer original. According to Psalm 139:14 NRSV, you are "fearfully and wonderfully made." Rejoice, celebrate, and express the gift of you!

Live in the Moment

Some of the greatest joys in life come unexpectedly. Far too often we miss them because our minds are somewhere else, either thinking about what happened in the past or perhaps worrying about what may happen in the future. Yet life is full of special moments designed to bring laughter, smiles, and even tears of joy. Learn to enjoy the moment; you will be pleasantly surprised by just how much joy is contained therein.

Every Dog Has Its Day

Resist the temptation to seek retribution or to execute judgment when you feel as though you have been wronged. There is a universal law that what goes around comes around. You may not be around to witness it, and perhaps it is better for you if you don't! But when you've been dogged, just remember that every dog indeed has its day.

Never Lend What You Can't Afford to Lose

It stands to reason that people borrow money because they do not have it. Realistically speaking, if they had it, there would be no need to borrow it. Therefore, it is ill advised to lend money under the pretense that the borrower will be able to pay it back. Consider it a gift, and if they pay it back, consider it a blessing.

Swim with the Tide

It is extremely difficult to swim upstream. Rest assured that our goals are far more easily achieved when we swim with, rather than against, the tide. I love going to the beach and occasionally braving the waters. I have learned that when I have the misfortune of getting caught in a current, the quickest way to safety is to swim with the current rather than against it. When we embrace the struggle and learn to go with the flow, we are more likely to reach our destination and enjoy the journey while en route.

Life's Most Precious Moments Are Often Unplanned

In this age of day planners, apps, software, and the myriad of other tools available to keep us on task, on point, and on schedule, spontaneity often becomes the first casualty of our busy lives. And yet, most of life's most delightful, memorable, and precious moments are unplanned. Every now and then, it pays to throw the schedule out the window. Do something spontaneous, and enjoy yourself while you are at it.

Root, Little Pig, or Die

If you have ever witnessed a litter of piglets at feeding time, you know it is a sight to see. All the piglets attempt at the same time to get access to their mother's teats (rooting), their source of nourishment. It is quite a competition. If a little piglet is not assertive enough, it can compromise its seat at the table when feeding time comes and miss out on the life-sustaining nourishment. Similarly, in our lives, for us to successfully achieve our goals and dreams, we too must take an assertive posture to dig in and go after the things that nourish and sustain our dreams. No matter how fierce the competition, make sure you are intentional about securing your seat at the table of life.

Play the Hand That Was Dealt You

You can either complain about your situation, or you can decide to cease complaining and work with what you have and make the best of it. You just may find that when you concentrate on what you have rather than focusing on what others have, you are in a better situation than you think. Focus on what's in *your* hand.

The Road to Perfection Is Always under Construction

We should never cease to develop our gifts and to hone our crafts and skills. We may reach a level of mastery in a specific area, but we should refrain from the thought or perception that we are, or ever will be, perfect. There is always an area that needs development, new lessons to learn, and new vistas to conquer. We are always striving to be better, but perfection is a goal that moves every time we move.

Self Is a Full-Time Job

Self-examination and evaluation are the best ways to resist delving into the lives and issues of others. If you focus on yourself, you will soon learn that your issues, challenges, and concerns are substantive enough to manage without considering others. Your stuff, alone, requires all your attention.

Dance Every Day like It's Your Last

Living life with gladness and dancing is a surefire method to chase the blues away. Each day is a gift, and celebrating it and embracing what it has to offer shows God gratitude. There is power in the dance that promotes wellness and brings about health and healing. You could say that a dance a day keeps the doctor away. Now dance on!

Small-Minded People Can't Make You Feel Bad, and Big-Minded People Won't Try

It never feels good when people attempt to malign, tarnish, or taint your name, especially when you are undeserving. Just remember that while they are building a case against you, they are also building a reputation for themselves as people who specialize in hitting below the belt. Keep in mind the model and motto of our beloved former first lady, Michelle Obama, who inspired us with the words "When they go low, we go high!" It will surely keep your reputation and your heart intact.

CHAPTER 5

LITTLE THINGS

Even a Dog Will Wag Its Tail

There is something about a warm greeting that can change the countenance of a familiar soul and even an unknown stranger. All too often we are so absorbed in ourselves that we fail to acknowledge those in our presence. It is a polite practice to greet folks when you enter their presence or when they enter yours. Dogs wag; people should at least wave!

Step on a Dog's Tail, and It Will Holla

You will often find that the guilty people in any given situation are usually the first to defend and the loudest in their expression of offense. They are both loud *and* wrong. Just know that if you give them enough space they will almost always tell on themselves. Wait for it—just wait for it!

Every Crow Thinks Theirs Is the Blackest

I have fond memories of my mother and father glowing with great parental pride whenever I sang, preached, spoke, or did anything, really. They represented the best of my two-person fan club. One day as they were boosting my ego by telling me how amazing I was, I responded with the question "Really?" They replied, "Well, you know, every crow thinks theirs is the blackest."

A Watched Pot Never Boils

A surefire way for something to take forever is to sit, watch, and wait for it to happen. No matter how much you wish it to be so, it is going to happen when it happens. Just be patient; all things in time!

Can't Kill Nothing, and Nothing Won't Die

Hunters often use this expression after returning from an unproductive hunting trip. Metaphorically speaking, it essentially expresses the disappointment we feel when we fail at something or when our efforts are unsuccessful when attempting to accomplish goals. Whatever you do, don't allow the disappointments of life cause you to give up. In other words, "If at first you don't succeed, try and try again!"

A Well-Modulated Voice Is a Sure Sign of Culture

This was something that my father used to say to me when I insisted on using my outside voice inside. While there is a time and a place for everything, he wanted to impress upon me the importance of knowing the distinction between boisterousness and refinement. Moreover, he wanted me to have the wisdom to know to demonstrate poise when appropriate.

Don't Cry over Spilled Milk

We must learn to handle our disappointments with grace and finesse. On the journey of life, we will undoubtedly encounter challenges, rejection, disappointment, and even unpleasant situations and circumstances we cannot do anything about. The fact is that spilled milk is unsalvageable. Chalk it up as a loss, get over it, and move on.

Sometimes You're the Bug, and Sometimes You're the Windshield

It is important to acknowledge that in life, we will encounter situations and conflicts with no real favorable outcome. We may find ourselves choosing between two outcomes, realizing that in the end, there is no real winner. Even when the bug crashes and pays the ultimate price, the windshield doesn't come out of the situation squeaky clean.

Nothing Beats a Failure but a Try

Failure is sometimes difficult to handle. It can be painful and disappointing to fail at anything. However, we must be careful to ensure that we don't let failure stop us. We can't succeed at anything we aren't willing to try. Failure wins by default. Whenever we make the effort, we are well on our pathway to succeeding.

A Hard Head Makes a Soft Behind

These words are often used by parents to their young ones as a warning that if their acts of disobedience and defiance continue, a spanking on their hind parts is sure to follow. The warning is still befitting for adults, metaphorically speaking. We would see how much easier the way would be if we learned from our mistakes the first time around and humbly received the lessons life is seeking to teach us.

Monkey See, Monkey Do

You have probably noticed that whenever you are around someone for an extended period, you begin to pick up their mannerisms, habits, and behavior. Mimicry oftentimes happens at a very subconscious level and is not necessarily a bad thing, particularly if you are in good company. However, be advised—thoughtful and discerning consideration should always be given before repeating the actions of another. Ultimately, trust your own mind and inner voice to guide you down the right path.

Pretty Is as Pretty Does

A person may be wonderfully attractive on the outside, and yet his or her attitude, disposition, and temperament leave a lot to be desired. You are only as beautiful as your behavior dictates.

Act Your Age and Not Your Shoe Size

No matter how big your feet are or what size shoe you wear, the number is comparable to the age range for juveniles. Please ensure that your actions, behaviors, and attitudes reflect the sensibilities of an adult and not the immaturity of a child.

Don't Make a Mountain
out of a Molehill

Things happen along life's journey, including heartbreak, trials, and disappointments both big and small. One must avoid the tendency to claim every situation is a catastrophe, particularly those of smaller proportion. While mountains are momentous, molehills are minuscule by comparison. Take care not to make the circumstance larger than it really is.

SECTION 2

LOVE

Love Is Caught

When we catch the flu or another virus, it often comes unexpectedly, with little warning. One minute you are okay, and the next thing you know symptoms start and you realize you are coming down with a bug. So it is with love. It can sneak up on you when you are neither looking for it nor expect it, and—*boom!*—there it is. You've been bitten by the love bug!

With Every Goodbye You Learn

It has been said that some relationships are for a lifetime, while others come into our lives for a specific reason or a specific season. The handwriting is on the wall when the relationship becomes one-sided or a burden and no longer brings you joy. When it's time to say goodbye, say goodbye. Make sure you glean from the experience and cherish the lessons learned.

Start Out like You Can Hold Out

I once asked my mother for a bead of wisdom, and her response was short, sweet, and quite profound. She simply stated, "Start out like you can hold out." Before we start anything, it is important to consider our ability to sustain it. The worst thing we can do is to create an expectation that we cannot meet or to overpromise and underdeliver. Determining up front if we can keep it up for the long haul will make for a much happier relationship.

If You Pick and Choose, the Best You'll Refuse

Sometimes the greatest gifts in life are right in front of us and well within our reach. Unfortunately, we often miss out on the best choice because we are too busy looking over and around it in a quest for whatever it is we think we want. All the while, what we truly need is staring us right in the face. Be careful you don't miss it!

Kisses Aren't Contracts

In matters of the heart, don't be too gullible. Instead of jumping in with both feet, take it one step at a time and one day at a time. See where things go and if they grow. Remember that a hug is a hug, not a commitment, and a kiss is just a kiss; neither is necessarily a contract. If it's the real thing, time will show it and you will know it.

There Is Just as Good a Fish in the Sea That Has Ever Been Caught Out

When love relationships go sour, as they sometimes do, say a graceful goodbye. Even if you think you had a good catch, always remember there are many good fish in the sea. Just like you caught that one, you'll catch the next!

Still Waters Run Deep

It is ill advised when you encounter people who are not very talkative to assume they don't have anything on their minds. People who are quiet are not necessarily shallow; they may very well be profound and much deeper than you think.

SECTION 3

LEADERSHIP

People Love Success, but They Loathe Successful People

Sad but true. People love to experience the fruit of the success of others but unfortunately, some find it hard to celebrate them for their accomplishments. While it may be disheartening at times, try not to take it personally. It's a flaw that comes with the territory. Don't get lost in the chatter. Just keep your eyes on the prize and keep moving forward!

If It Ain't Broke, Don't Fix It

Change is not a four-letter word and is often necessary for progress to take place. However, there is an art to managing change. It should be incremental, gradual, and effectively communicated to all stakeholders. If not handled properly, change can have an adverse effect. Avoid change just for change's sake. If something isn't broken, there is no need to try to fix it.

Trust but Verify

This phrase was coined by Ronald Reagan, the fortieth president of the United States. Among the many things he will be remembered for, this is one of his most enduring legacies. It is great to be able to trust but far better to be able to verify.

There Is Always a More Excellent Way

No matter how familiar you are with a task or a way of doing something, strive to approach every situation with a fresh perspective. There may be a better way of accomplishing what is before you. Always have a listening ear, embrace the counsel of trusted advisers and confidants, and remain open to the opinions of others that may differ from yours. By seeing things with new eyes, you may discover new and better ways of doing old things.

Inspect What You Expect

Experience has taught me that no matter how plain we think we have made the vision, how clear the direction, or how detailed the instructions, something is always subject to get lost in translation. Don't ever take the intended outcome for granted; always inspect what you expect.

Familiarity Breeds Contempt

Wisdom dictates that relationship parameters should always be respected, particularly when professional in nature. Oftentimes, when we encounter people who are good-natured and easy to be around, we can develop a level of comfort that can lead to familiarity. Unfortunately, familiarity can blur the boundaries, making it difficult to give and receive critique, correction, and discipline. It can make for a very contemptable situation if the relationship is not kept in the proper perspective.

Be Determined to Finish Well

Studies have shown that only a third of gifted leaders who are chosen for greatness finish well. Many start out well, but the journey often goes downhill from there. To achieve our goals and God-given assignments in life, we must be diligent, disciplined, and determined to do so, seeking the wisdom of God to guide us through the stumbling blocks and pitfalls en route to our purpose.

When You Stop Learning, You Stop Living

One of the commonalities of those who have been successful in life, love, and labor is that they all made the commitment to be lifelong learners. Having a teachable spirit is essential to real growth and maturation. Commit to being a lifelong learner; it will yield much fruit!

WORKS CITED

American Heritage Dictionary of the English Language. 5th ed. s.v. "wisdom." Houghton Mifflin Harcourt Publishing Company, 2016.

Dictionary.com. s.v. "wit." https://www.dictionary.com/browse/wit?s=t.

Riggio, Ronald E. "There's Magic in Your Smile." *Psychology Today,* last modified June 25, 2012. https://www.psychologytoday.com/us/blog/cutting-edge-leadership/201206/there-s-magic-in-your-smile.

Back Cover Photo, ©Fond Memories Photography, Jackie Hicks.

CPSIA information can be obtained
at www.ICGtesting.com
Printed in the USA
FSHW022224220419
57487FS